SWATI SENGUPTA is an author and former journalist. Her books include *Out of War* (Speaking Tiger Books, 2016), *Guns on My Red Earth* (Rupa, 2013), *Half the Field Is Mine* (Scholastic, 2014), *The Talking Bird* (Tulika Books, 2014) and *A Tea Garden Party* (Pratham Books, 2021). She translated *Murder in the City* (Speaking Tiger Books, 2018) from Bengali to English. Swati runs a workshop series on gender for young adults. She studied English at Jadavpur University and lives in Kolkata.

Also in the series by Swati Sengupta:

Jhalkari Bai: The Braveheart Warrior

Milkha Singh: The Runner Who Could Fly

Birsa Munda: The Great Revolutionary Leader

Savitribai Phule: The Fearless Reformer

Arati Saha: The Swimmer Who Wouldn't Give Up

Bhagat Singh: The Indomitable Freedom Fighter

Anandibai Joshee: The Girl Who Fought to Be a Doctor

The Incredible Life of

Satyendranath Bose

A Great Scientist of the World

Swati Sengupta

Illustrations by
Devashish Verma

talking CUB
An Imprint of Speaking Tiger Books

TALKING CUB

Published by Speaking Tiger Books LLP
125A, Ground Floor, Shahpur Jat,
Near Asiad Village, New Delhi 110 049

First published in paperback in Talking Cub
by Speaking Tiger Books in 2024

ISBN: 978-93-5447-987-8

eISBN: 978-93-5447-910-6

10 9 8 7 6 5 4 3 2 1

Typeset in Georgia by Jojy Philip
Printed at HT Media Ltd, Greater Noida

To Tapas Sen

Chapter One

Surendranath Bose was on his way back from the market with the fish and the vegetables. He was filled with child-like excitement. He could not wait to see what his son Satyen would be doing. Once he got home, he quickly changed and rushed off to check on his son. He opened the door to the store room a wee bit, and peeped inside.

A little boy of four, lost in a sea of numbers, was sitting amid stacks of pulses, lentils, oil, soap, sugar, salt, old beddings, pillows and old

clothes. Dressed in shorts and a vest, the boy was poring over numbers, staring at them in wonderment. Numbers and math symbols had been scrawled in chalk on the red cement floor of the room. Satyen was looking delighted as he stared at the numbers and added more on the shiny red floor.

'Wonderful!' Surendranath exclaimed. 'You got everything correct! Was it tough?'

Little Satyen giggled. 'Mathematics isn't tough, Baba. Please give me some really difficult sums next time you go out. I finish them so fast.' Then, excited, he added, 'Look, Baba! The red floor looks like a pond and the numbers and symbols seem to be swimming in it.'

Satyen, whose pet name was Bodi, named after the deity Baidyanath, had a special love for numbers. Every time Surendranath left home for some work, he assigned mathematics problems for the child to solve. Often, he told little Satyen to solve them on the floor, just to make it more fun and innovative. Doing sums in exercise books would seem like studying, but the same sums done on the floor would make it feel like a game. A proud Surendranath wondered if he should introduce some new concepts to the boy. The child seemed to be picking up maths so fast and got bored when there was nothing new to learn.

Little Satyen, or Satyendranath Bose, had started going to Normal School, close to their house in Calcutta. Born on 1 January 1894, Satyen was the eldest child of Surendranath and Amodini. It wasn't very long ago that the family had moved to Calcutta (now Kolkata), the capital of British colonial government in India at that time.

Surendranath worked as an accountant in the East India Railways in the executive engineering department. He had to struggle hard with many responsibilities that came one after the other on his shoulders. He was a well-read man with diverse interests in literature and the sciences. He even set up a small pharmaceutical company with a partner in 1901, called Indian Chemical and Pharmaceutical Works.

Six more children were born to the couple after Satyen—all of them girls. The family eventually moved to their Ishwar Mill Lane house. Satyen was later admitted to the New Indian School. With every passing day, Surendranath became aware of his son's unusual intelligence and talent with numbers. He himself had once wanted to pursue a career in academics, but could not do so due to family responsibilities.

Satyen's eyesight was weak, but he overcame this disadvantage by memorising anything he had read just once or even just glimpsed. He got bored easily unless fresh challenges of difficult mathematics problems were thrown at him. His parents would wonder often if they would be able to give him the right opportunities.

The 'problem' was resolved when Surendranath decided to admit his son to the Hindu School. Here, he would study with the brightest and the best and face competition that would encourage him to do better.

What were schools like in India then?

Before the British ruled India, primary schools in Bengal taught simple arithmetic, Sanskrit and Bengali language, some grammar and literature and so on. Then, thanks to reformer Raja Rammohan Roy, there was a major social and cultural movement that took place in Bengal that came to be known as the Bengal Renaissance.

Raja Rammohan Roy and others like him felt there was a need for good quality institutions to spread education and to bring much needed changes in society. In 1815, Roy formed the Atmiya Sabha. It was a philosophical circle in which people discussed and debated various issues. An educationist, David Hare, proposed the setting up of an educational institution that would help bring about sweeping changes. That's how the idea of Hindu School and College came about.

At a meeting on 21 May 1816, it was decided that a school would be set up for boys of upper class Indians (Hindus), and they would be taught English language, literature and science, Bengali language and grammar, mathematics and so on. More than rupees one lakh was raised through donations for the purpose.

On 20 January 1817, twenty male students from various affluent families attended the first class of the Hindu School. People felt the powerful impact almost immediately, and many rushed to get their boys admitted. The other school of great repute during that time was Hare School, set up in 1818 by David Hare.

Satyendranath Bose was admitted to Hindu School in 1907. He was lucky to have parents who wanted him to get the best opportunities available.

Chapter Two

Satyen was gifted with a photographic memory—he hardly forgot what he had once seen. The longer the poem, the more he loved reciting it! One favourite was Alfred Tennyson's 'In Memoriam'.

Literature was his favourite, though he also loved music. But undoubtedly his first love was mathematics. And now that he was going to a new school, Satyen felt he had to prove himself before all his classmates and teachers. It was especially tough to impress the maths teacher

Upendranath Bakshi. Satyen worked hard, determined to ace his tests. Once, he wrote his answers in a test and was sure Upen babu would not be able to find any fault in the paper.

The day the corrected answer papers were to be handed out, a huge surprise was waiting for him. As the bell rang, Satyen's ears longed to hear Upen babu say that he had scored full marks. How proud his parents would be! With what admiration his classmates would look at him—the new boy in class!

One by one, Upen babu called out the names of those who had scored full marks. Satyen waited for his turn, but the teacher did not mention him. He began to feel jittery, and a cloud of doubt filled him. Had Sir made a mistake? Satyen was sure he had not made any! The teacher returned all the answer sheets. Each of his classmates was engrossed in their respective answer sheet while Satyen shuffled his feet.

Had Sir lost his answer script? As he wondered what to do, and whether he should tell *mastermoshai* that he was yet to receive his answer paper, Upendranath Bakshi announced something:

'Is Satyendranath Bose here?' The teacher's eyes darted across the room though Satyen knew that Sir had seen him earlier. What was all this about? Had he made some terrible mistake?

Satyen stood up.

'How much do you think you have scored?' Upendranath Bakshi asked. There was only one answer script on the desk before him. Satyen wasn't sure what to say. He was supposed to get full marks. Yet, had he scored cent per cent correct, he would not be singled out like this. Eyes downcast, Satyen did not say a word.

'I will tell you. In fact, I want to tell the whole class that Satyendranath Bose got 110 out of 100 marks. Should I repeat it?' Upen Bakshi said. Satyen's heart skipped a beat. Had he heard it right? How was it possible to score ten extra marks? The eyes of his classmates were wide with surprise. How was it possible?

The maths teacher explained to the class that Satyen's paper had been perfect. Not only were all the sums correct, the student had also meticulously worked out the solutions in all the alternative methods possible for each sum. It was due to this that the teacher had to go out of the way to give credit for this uncharacteristic talent.

‘What could I do? I had to give him more than full marks!’ Upen Bakshi said, a rare, mischievous smile playing on his lips.

From that day, Satyen was the star in his class, and Upendranath Bakshi had no doubt that the boy would do something remarkable someday.

He was spot-on! Satyendranath Bose did become a world renowned scientist. But for years, he was remembered as the boy who had once scored 110 out of 100 in mathematics!

~

After spending a year at the new school, it was time for Satyen to sit for the entrance examination in 1908. But he came down with a bout of fever and chicken pox. Sick and disappointed, Satyen realized that he would not be able to write the examination. This meant only one thing: he would have to appear for the exam the following year.

His parents had an idea, and Satyen could not help but agree. 'It's best to not get bored studying the same thing over and over again,' his father said.

'Why not read something else?' his mother suggested, giving him a book of poetry. The sting of the chicken pox eruptions all over Satyen's body felt a lot more tolerable once he lay on the bed and kept reading one book after another. Soon, piles of books stood like a multi-storied building inside his mosquito net as he slept, ate and read for the next few weeks. When he felt better, he managed to sit up and work on some mathematics. Three weeks flew by, and so did the following year.

Satyen sat for the entrance examinations in 1909. He stood fifth in the exams and opted to study science. His father had huge expectations from him, and he did not want any more time to be wasted. Satyen was a loyal and affectionate son who tried hard never to disappoint his parents.

Around this time, someone new appeared in Satyen's life.

'I must have seen you in our neighbourhood,' said one of the boys in his school.

'I live on Ishwar Mill Lane. You?' asked Satyen.

'Haralal Mitra Street. That's not far from your place,' said the boy. 'Want to come over to my house after school? My father has lots of books at home.'

'Really?' Satyen's eyes sparkled with joy.

'Yes, it's like a library,' the boy said.

And thus began a friendship in 1908 that lasted through their lives. Satyen started visiting the home of Girijapati Bhattacharjee. They discussed books and their various interests. One day, Satyen said they must try and 'construct' some instruments at home.

'What instruments?' Girija asked.

'How about a telescope?' said Satyen.

It was a great idea. And so, over the following days, they worked with small magnifying lenses. 'Will you be able to fix the lenses to a metal stand?' Satyen asked.

Girija made a face. 'I don't think so.'

So they assigned the work to a tin-smith in the neighbourhood. Tin-smiths were easily available and visited homes regularly to do sundry jobs. A few days later, Satyen went to Girija's house again, when the tin-smith was scheduled to visit.

With detailed instructions from Satyen and Girija, the magnifying lens was attached to a rod. 'Bravo! Tres bien, monsieur!' Satyen told the tin-smith, who gawped at him without making sense of what the boy was saying.

'What does that mean?' Girija asked.

'In French, it means very good, Sir,' Satyen said. He had been taking French language tuitions from a teacher and had learned the language quite well by then.

Their telescope gave about six to seven times magnification though the images were quite distorted. Yet, the boys were wild with excitement on doing something innovative!

Over the next few months, the duo made more new machines and devices. A battery-lit pocket lamp was set up with a lot of difficulty. While it did light up, the power was weak. It flickered and fluttered till the glow fizzled out in a few moments. Girija and Satyen looked at each other—should they be happy or sad? In the end, they burst out laughing. The joy of creation kept growing. Excited with two great successes, they wanted to try out more.

'How about making coal gas?' Satyen suggested.

'That would be great!' Girijapati's eyes glowed with excitement. So they got coal balls from the kitchen in Girija's home and put them in an earthenware. That was the safest container, which they covered as tightly as they could and lit a fire. As the gas formed and gathered in the container, the two young scientists were thrilled to bits!

Girija's brother Pashupati was also close to Satyen. After all, Satyen spent hours in their house. It was like a library of sorts, stacked with books on various subjects.

Another close friend of Satyen during his school days was Maniklal De. His house was also close by, on Beadon Street. Maniklal's family was known to the Tagore family and sometimes—when they were older—he would take Satyen to Rabindranath Tagore's house in Jorasanko.

In the entrance examination, Satyen and Maniklal got the same marks and stood fifth. In the Intermediate examination Satyen stood first and Maniklal came second. They were drawn to different subjects for the Bachelors though—Satyen opted for Mixed (or Applied) Mathematics and Maniklal chose Chemistry.

Intermediate courses existed in undivided Bengal and thereafter. During Satyendranath Bose's time, it was taught in colleges for two years after students completed their school-leaving examinations. Students could opt to study Science or Humanities. This was followed by undergraduate and post-graduate studies in colleges and universities. Bose studied Intermediate Science in Presidency College from 1909 to 1911. Then he completed his B.Sc. (Bachelor of Science) in 1913 and M.Sc. (Master of Science) in 1915.

Satyen's schooldays, college years and the years spent in Calcutta thereafter, were filled with wonderful time with friends and many exciting events. He even attended the Vichitra Club programmes at Calcutta's Jorasanko on 6/4 Dwarka Nath Lane, within the premises of the house of the Tagores, the family of Rabindranath Tagore. This club was founded in 1915 by the Tagore family. Vichitra, meaning 'various', was a platform that explored different styles and methods of painting and printmaking, and held discussions on art and literature. It was considered an important cultural institution in the Calcutta of early twentieth century.

Chapter Three

Satyen joined the Intermediate Science classes at Presidency College, Calcutta, in 1909. He studied up to M.Sc. from this college. There was tough competition as there were several outstanding students in his batch. There were brilliant students in senior batches as well, and many more would join Presidency over the next few years. All of them were remarkable, and it was a mix of talent and hard work that made them so successful not just in India, but internationally too, in their respective fields of work.

The faculty in Presidency included some of the biggest names in the fields of science and mathematics, none other than the renowned scientist Jagadish Chandra Bose, who taught Satyen in college.

Jagadish Chandra Bose had returned from the UK and joined Presidency as a professor of physics in 1885. In 1895, at a dramatic public demonstration at Town Hall in Calcutta, he had sent electromagnetic waves through walls to make a bell ring and to cause a tiny explosion with gunpowder! He did not stick to one subject—he was a polymath who worked in various fields such as biology, physics, medicine and even wrote science fiction!

Another eminent faculty of Presidency at this time was Prafulla Chandra Ray. He had returned from the UK and joined the Chemistry department. In 1892, he founded the Bengal Chemical & Pharmaceutical Works, a research and production unit for indigenous medicines. It was a big success story in creating some outstanding natural products that were of excellent quality that stood the test of time. It is known as India's first chemical and pharmaceutical company.

Surendranath Maitra taught physics, D.N. Mallick, Shyamadas Mukherjee and C.E. Cullis taught mathematics and Manmohan Ghosh taught English—they were some of the renowned teachers of those times.

Satyen took physiology as a subject and it was taught by Professor Subodh Mahalanobis, who was a pioneer in India in the study of the mechanism of cells, organs and organ systems.

Some of the brightest students were there, too. Jnan Chandra Ghosh, who later came to be known for his contribution to scientific research, industrial development and technology education in India, and served as the director of the institute that later became IIT Kharagpur. Jnanendra Nath Mukherjee, who became a renowned chemist known for his major work on colloids (colloids are somewhat like mixtures, and have specific properties. They are tiny particles of matter dispersed throughout another matter) was there as well.

Satyen's seniors included P.C. Mahalanobis, a pioneer in the field of statistics who did pathbreaking work in anthropometry (study of assessing size, proportion and composition of the human body) and in analysing large-scale sample surveys. He also set up the Indian Statistical Institute in Calcutta. Others included Nilratan Dhar, who did pioneering work in thermal and photochemical fixation of atmospheric nitrogen in soil, and S.K. Mitra, a brilliant physicist known for his work on the ionosphere.

Many wonder how so many brilliant minds were growing and flourishing in the same place at the same time—Calcutta of the late 19th and early 20th century. In his book, *The Geography of Genius: A Search for the World's Most Creative Places from Ancient Athens to Silicon Valley,* Eric Weiner wrote: 'Certain places, at certain times, produced a bumper crop of brilliant minds and good ideas.' He chose Calcutta of 1840 to 1920 in the list of these places. This is when some of the brightest and the best brains created some of the greatest scientific research works. Some had already taken great strides, while others would soon follow and reach unbelievable heights.

The years of Intermediate studies, Bachelors and Masters from Presidency College were eventful. Imagine being taught by Prafulla Chandra Ray and Jagadish Chandra Bose! The students were star-struck and gaped at these teachers when they saw them either in class while they were teaching or when they were in their office rooms in college poring over documents at their desk or working on some experiment.

Prafulla Chandra Ray was a brilliant teacher and an outstanding storyteller. He narrated dramatic tales of scientific inventions and the lives of famous scientists.

Through these inspiring and magnificent stories, the students easily learned about great innovations, and the unique ways in which some of the major findings of the past few decades came about.

Ray told the boys stories of Louis Pasteur, the French chemist and microbiologist known for his work in vaccination, microbial fermentation and most importantly, pasteurisation. He told them about John Dalton, the English chemist, physicist and meteorologist known for his work on atomic theory in chemistry and findings on colour blindness. He also narrated to them experiments by the Swedish chemist Jons Jacob Berzelius, one of the founders of modern chemistry.

Many thought that Ray with his bearded, saintly appearance, would be very serious and devoid of humour. But nothing could be further from the truth. Students listened to these stories in awe and word spread about his classes far and wide. His boisterous way of teaching made him hugely popular. Students from other colleges would attend Ray's classes, too, the room choc-a-block with pupils, listening intently to the genius. Satyen was lucky to get a teacher like Ray right from his Intermediate classes.

Acharya Prafulla Chandra Ray liked to tickle the funny bone during his classes. Once he asked the orderly Sitaram to come to his class. Then he gave him a tight hug to explain to his students: 'This is how molecules attract each other!'

Satyen was a mischievous child in school, and had carried this streak to college. It was this attitude that made Ray call him to the front of the class, asking him to sit by his side to prevent Satyen from 'disturbing' everyone. And voila! It actually worked in Satyen's favour. Having a weak eyesight, he was able to read the board better and have a clearer view of the experiments!

Chapter Four

One of the biggest stars of Presidency College was Jagadish Chandra Bose. He was to be seen mostly engrossed in his work or quietly thinking. Though from outside he did not seem to have a great connect with students, the boys all gazed at him in amazement whenever he passed by. Every Indian knew about his research work. He was a known figure nationally and internationally.

Born in 1858 in Bikrampur of present-day Bangladesh, Jagadish Chandra Bose is one of the greatest scientists the world has seen, with pathbreaking findings in physical and biological sciences.

He had been to London to study medicine but could not pursue it due to health reasons, and studied science at Christ's College, Cambridge. Later, he also received a B.Sc. degree from University of London. He returned to India and became professor of physics in Presidency College. He continued with his research in a number of areas. He created a version of the coherer, a detecting device for radio waves. He publicly demonstrated this in 1895. He also created a device called the crescograph, that recorded the growth of plants and used it to understand various reactions in plants to different stimuli.

He founded the Bose Institute in Calcutta in 1917. His books include the renowned *Response in the Living and Non-Living* (1902) and *The Nervous Mechanism of Plants* (1926). He also wrote science fiction. A crater on the moon is named after him.

Satyen, like many others, would watch Acharya Jagadish Chandra Bose when he was working on his wireless experiments in his glass-walled office room. 'Are we now witnessing some great experiment at work that the world will come to

know in the next few years? Isn't that a wonderful privilege?' Satyen would tell Maniklal or Girija.

'It is like a temple of science, Girija,' Satyen said. 'Turn left, see Acharya Jagadish Chandra Bose; turn right and see Acharya Prafulla Chandra Ray. Let us not forget where we are walking through,' he added.

Satyen spent a lot of time at his friend Girijapati's home during his college days. In fact, he had his first musical training in this house. This is where he often played the *esraj*. The esraj is an Indian stringed instrument played with a bow, with features of the sarangi and sitar. Its sound is intrinsically connected with Rabindrasangeet—the songs composed by Rabindranath Tagore. With time, Satyen became rather good at it. He also played the flute. Girijapati's brother Pashupati sang wonderfully, and in this house the three of them had frequent and long musical sessions.

When it was time for the examination results, there were no surprises. It was the beginning of a winning streak for Satyendranath Bose. He obtained first position in Intermediate Science. Meghnad Saha, who would become another bright star in the scientific field, joined Presidency College for a B.Sc., and Satyendranath and Meghnad chose Applied (Mixed) Mathematics. This was the beginning of another long-lasting friendship.

Meghnad Saha was a pioneering astrophysicist from India who developed the Saha ionization equation. He was born in 1893 in Seoratali near Dhaka of present-day Bangladesh. The equation named after him is a mathematical relationship between the observed spectra of stars and their temperatures. Saha's research involved a wide range of subjects, including the age of rocks. He was behind the formation of many scientific institutes across India. The Saha Institute of Nuclear Physics was founded in 1949 in Calcutta, and named after him. He died in 1956.

In 1913, the B.Sc. (Honours) results were out. Satyen stood first, Meghnad second, and Nikhilranjan came third. After two years–in 1915–it was time for the Masters results and again Satyen stood first, and Meghnad second.

Apart from his friendship with Girija and Maniklal, Satyen also had close ties with Meghnad Saha and Jnan Ghosh. They were joined together in affection, camaraderie, and fierce competition! Who was the best? This question played in the minds of all three as they shared notes, and planned to do great things in the future.

While still a student, Satyen got married at the age of twenty, to Ushabati, the daughter of a renowned doctor. Satyen was devoted to his parents and agreed to marry, even though he was very young, and Ushabati even younger. She was then only eleven years old.

Ushabati took an instant liking to the young man who, she had heard, was very good in his studies. He seemed gentle and kind and always engrossed in reading. He told Ushabati that he would teach her the English language. They bonded over this and over his many wonderful dreams for the future. Ushabati was confident that Satyen would achieve it. They had a daughter right after his Masters. They named her Nilima. Over the years, they had nine children and suffered great anguish on losing two of them. Through joys and pain, Satyen and Ushabati supported each other.

Once the Masters results were declared, everyone around was proud of Satyen and Meghnad's success. But it wasn't smooth sailing for the two toppers of the Mixed Mathematics batch. Both had to struggle for at least a year as no jobs were available. They began to offer private tuitions. Meghnad had to support his family back home in Dhaka, and in Calcutta he had to earn for himself and his brother who was studying in college. All day he was on a bicycle crisscrossing the city to earn a few rupees. Satyen was married and needed to find a job desperately, or get a scholarship to travel to Europe for research work. But he met with all kinds of difficulties—he was either turned down for being 'overqualified' and sometimes his outspokenness stood in the way.

~

Around this time, an important development was taking place in the field of science in Calcutta, thanks to Sir Ashutosh Mukherjee, the Vice Chancellor of the University of Calcutta. Barrister Taraknath Palit and Dr Nilratan Sircar came together to form a technical institute. However, this did not seem to have many takers. Palit then handed over his donations to Sir Ashutosh Mukherjee.

The University College of Science (UCS) was founded on 27 March 1914, by Sir Ashutosh Mukherjee, using donations from Sir Taraknath Palit and Sir Rashbehari Ghosh. They had together donated nearly Rs 37.5 lakh and the premises.

Apart from Satyen and Meghnad, their friend Sailen Ghosh too was without a job. He thought of various possibilities of approaching Sir Ashutosh, and then one day, he had an idea! He proposed to Sir Ashutosh to introduce subjects in the UCS that were not taught at Presidency. A meeting was fixed for all of them to meet Sir Ashutosh.

Sir Ashutosh Mukherjee was an eminent mathematician himself. His position and aura made him somewhat intimidating for young persons. He had learnt that the young generation was keen to take up new subjects at the university level. And so his first question to the young men was: 'So, what are the subjects you consider yourself competent to teach?'

'We will try to the best of our capacities whatever you ask us to teach, Sir,' Satyen and Meghnad almost said together. A hint of a smile appeared on Sir Ashutosh's face.

Only a few Indians at that time had travelled abroad for research and the Indian students here were not yet acquainted with scientific research and progress taking place around the world, especially in Germany. They knew about Max Planck, Albert Einstein, Neils Bohr's pathbreaking work but they needed to study these. Due to the First World War, books or journals on these scientific works could not be brought to India. The books available were in German, limited copies were available, and only a few knew the language. No English translations were available yet even of Einstein's famous work.

The good thing was that Meghnad knew German, and Satyen knew French and he had started learning German already.

They got their first big opportunity from Sir Ashutosh. They were offered a special allowance of Rs 125 each, per month. They were to learn all the latest developments in modern physics. But where would they get access to these books and journals?

It was a lucky coincidence that someone like P.J. Brühl, a German teacher, was living close to

Calcutta at that time. Brühl taught at the Bengal Engineering College, Shibpur (though its name was different then). He had a fabulous library stacked with the latest books and journals on science, particularly physics. He had studied botany but poor health had led him to change his research area to physics and move to India for the warm climate. Brühl and Sir Ashutosh's libraries provided the duo with plenty of study material.

Another friend, Debendramohan Bose, who had got his PhD from Berlin University and returned to India in July 1919, helped Satyen and Meghnad with books and information. He also helped Satyen to sharpen his German language skills. Debendramohan Bose was in Germany for many years and had got the golden opportunity to listen to talks by Planck and Einstein among others.

It was time for an extraordinary partnership between Satyen and Meghnad.

Chapter Five

In 1905, Albert Einstein wrote a series of four papers that changed the way we look at the universe.

In 1918, after Satyendranath Bose and Meghnad Saha collaborated on some papers, they began to translate the original relativity papers of Albert Einstein. They decided to do this for students who did not know German, as no English translation of Einstein's papers had been done till then.

This became a huge turnaround in Satyendranath Bose's career. He found a new path emerging before him. But who was this great scientist, Albert Einstein?

~

Albert Einstein is considered to be one of the greatest scientists the world has ever seen. He was born on 14 March 1879, in Ulm, Germany. The family moved to Munich and his father operated a small electrical and engineering plant. When Albert was two years old, his sister Maja was born. Their mother Pauline

was an outstanding pianist, and Albert's love of music came from her.

As a child, Einstein was very quiet, and his parents sometimes wondered whether he was just 'too' quiet. It is said that Albert did not speak till he was about three years old. However, this very fact was seen later by some as a rather good thing, as it meant Albert thought in concepts rather than in words.

Albert's life changed dramatically at four or five years old, when his father gifted him a magnetic compass. He was fascinated by it. Little Albert wondered at the swinging needle inside, shook the compass repeatedly, turned it upside down in his attempt to figure out how it worked. This was the key impetus that attracted him towards physics.

The family moved to Milan, and Albert continued his education in Switzerland. Albert was brilliant in physics, maths, Greek and Latin and in playing the violin. He wrote an academic paper when he was just sixteen years old!

In 1896, he entered the Swiss Federal Polytechnic School in Zurich to train as a teacher in physics and maths. He got his diploma in 1901, and a Swiss citizenship, but was not able to find a job as a teacher. Then he got a job in Bern as a technical assistant in the Swiss Patent Office and he moved there in 1902. He worked on his theories in his spare time. In 1905, he got his doctoral degree. This year is often called Albert's 'Year of Miracles' because that is when he published four pathbreaking papers, including the famous formula $E = mc^2$.

In these papers he said that matter—the tiny particles that form objects—can be turned into energy. He also showed the connection between mass and energy through the equation $E=mc^2$. It contributed to the development of quantum mechanics and provided a fundamental insight into reality.

He did all of this by the time he was only twenty-six years old!

Albert Einstein took up a teaching post at the University of Zurich in 1909. In 1911, he moved to Prague as a Professor of Theoretical Physics, and continued to publish papers. The following year, he returned to Federal Institute of Technology in Zurich as Professor. In 1914, he joined the University of Berlin. He remained in Berlin till 1933. By 1915, he completed his general theory of relativity. Einstein's work had helped topple the existing ideas of space and time and proposed a new understanding of gravity.

~

Einstein did not turn into an overnight sensation after the publication of his papers in 1905.

It took time for word to spread. And when the scientific community understood the significance of his work, ripples were felt all over the world. It was not only acknowledged and accepted, but the finding and the scientist himself became a superstar! Albert Einstein became a name to reckon with.

The impact of the finding was not just in the field of theoretical physics—the part of physics that deals in mathematical form on how the natural phenomena of the world and universe work—it also helped scientists after him work on new discoveries and findings based on the work.

Teachers and students around the world were trying to understand the theory of relativity, but this was tough as the world was going through difficult times. World War I happened between 1914 and 1918.

Einstein's work was available in the German language, and many were looking to read it in translations into languages they understood. One such person was Satyendranath Bose himself, who began to look for copies of his work in various libraries. When it was not available in the English language, Bose and his friend Meghnad Saha started translating it.

Albert Einstein won the Nobel Prize in Physics in 1921. After the theory of relativity, he continued to work for many years in various areas. He died in 1955 at the age of seventy-six.

~

When all these developments were taking place in Europe, many of Satyendranath and Meghnad Saha's classmates were there, chasing their dreams. But these two toppers were struggling and still nurturing their big dreams while working in Calcutta. Their English translation of Einstein's papers was published in 1920 by the University of Calcutta.

At times, Satyen felt frustrated.

He had some differences with Sir Ashutosh, and though these were not major issues, he now wanted to explore other things. After he had taught at the University College of Science in Calcutta for four years, Bose got an offer from Dacca (later Dhaka) University to join them as Reader in Experimental or Mathematical Physics. Invited by Sir Philip Joseph Hartog, the Vice Chancellor of the newly formed University of Dhaka, Satyendranath Bose decided that it was time to move on.

Chapter Six

From Calcutta, Bose took a train to Goalando, a small town in eastern India (now in Bangladesh) and from there a steamer took him to Narayangunj. Then, a train to Dhaka.

The university was located in Ramna, just outside Dhaka. It was a sprawling campus full of lush greenery. Satyen created a beautiful garden filled with flowers and fruits in front of his house. It was a delightful haven of calm.

When Satyendranath Bose settled down in Dhaka, Meghnad Saha was travelling in Europe, exploring the scientific progress that was occurring there. Satyen desperately missed his friends, especially Meghnad, with whom he had a deep connection over physics. In July 1921 he wrote to him:

> *My dear Meghnad,*
> *I have not heard from you for a long time... have you decided to boycott me for my irregular correspondence? Jnan and I are in the same place now. He tells me that you have been to Germany and met many stalwarts. I also heard that you were supposed to visit Munich. Can we expect a graphic account of your experience?*
> *Sayten*

Satyen Bose taught thermodynamics and Maxwell's electromagnetic theory in the B.Sc. and M.Sc. courses. Students found his classes

fascinating. After all, Bose considered himself more of a student than a teacher. He was hungry for knowledge, always looking to get his hands on the latest scientific development. He often spoke to his students regarding the many events taking place in Europe, particularly Germany, where scientists were coming together and making new progress every day.

Even as he was teaching, Satyen was studying Max Planck's *Thermodynamik* (Thermodynamics, published in 1897) and *Theorie der Warmestrahlung* (Theory of Heat and Radiation, published in 1906) again and again.

Max Planck was born on 23 April 1858 in Kiel, Schleswig (now Germany). He is known for his work on thermodynamics and radiation processes.

Planck's work is related to the relationship between energy and the frequency of radiation.

Calculations with then known laws of physics did not give convincing results, as it gave 'infinite' result. Planck solved this problem in 1900. He introduced the theory of 'quanta' and brought the concept of a fundamental constant, that came to be known as 'Planck's constant'.

One of Max Planck's two sons was executed for his role in an unsuccessful attempt to assassinate Adolf Hitler in 1944.

Planck died on 4 October 1947.

While he was studying Planck, Satyendranath Bose sought more clarity on certain aspects of his theory. Meghnad Saha came to visit him in Dhaka. Spending time together was like a breath of fresh air for both! They exchanged so much knowledge and filled each other with excitement about new findings and possibilities.

Satyen wanted to resolve some grey areas that remained during these discussions. 'There's a need to work out a derivation,' he told Meghnad.

He spent nights wide awake, staring at the starlit sky and working on calculations that seemed to lead him to a dead end. Frustrated, he kept thinking. Why was it turning out to be so tough? He was pretty close to a great idea, but the calculations weren't working out convincingly. At least not just yet. He knew only he could do it. It would be a mathematical calculation for sure, but it would require a deep, thorough understanding of physics. It wasn't easy, but whoever said great work happened easily?

And then, finally, he was able to work it out. Sitting at his desk, Satyen often wrote letters to his family and friends. Sometimes he spoke to his colleagues. During one of these conversations, he told a colleague: 'I have to explain many new ideas to the classes. I have to constantly study and update myself, and there are many new ideas in my head. I have written a paper synthesizing the basic principles of Planck's theory and Einstein's light-quantum (photon) hypothesis. I have written a paper and sent it for publication.'

In March-April 1924, Bose wrote the paper 'Planck's Law and the Light-Quantum Hypothesis' and sent it to *Philosophical Magazine*. He waited for a while to hear from them. Then, he wrote another paper called 'Thermal Equilibrium in the Radiation Field in the Presence of Matter'. He was so confident about the publication of the first paper, that he sent the second one with the footnote 'to appear in Phil Mag'. But there was no response. Satyen was getting restless and frustrated. He was confident that his finding was groundbreaking. What should he do now?

Finally, he decided that only a great mind would understand the value of his work. Who else but Albert Einstein? He would seek support from the only person whose approval mattered. He decided to send the paper to Albert Einstein.

On 4 June 1924, Satyendranth Bose sent a postal mail to Germany in which he inserted a copy of his first paper. It was addressed to Albert Einstein.

> *Respected Sir,*
>
> *I have ventured to send you the accompanying article for your perusal and opinion. I am anxious to know what you think of it... I do not know sufficient German to translate the paper. If you think the paper is worth publication, I shall be grateful if you arrange for its publication in* Zeitschrift für Physik. *Though a complete stranger to you, I do not feel any hesitation in*

making such a request. Because we are all your pupils though profiting only by your teachings through your writings. I do not know whether you still remember that somebody from Calcutta asked your permission to translate your papers on Relativity in English. You acceded to the request. The book has since been published. I was the one who translated your paper on Generalised Relativity.

Yours faithfully,
S.N. Bose

What arrived in the mailbox some weeks later startled him, though curiously, this is exactly what he had been expecting. It was a letter from Albert Einstein:

Dear Colleague,

I have translated your work and communicated it to Zeitschrift für Physik *for publication. It signifies an important step forward and I liked it very much. In fact I find your objection against my work not correct. For Wien's displacement law does not assume the wave (undulation) theory and Bohr's correspondence principle is not at all applicable. However, this does not matter. You are the first to derive the factor quantum theoretically, even though because of the polarization factor 2 not wholly rigorously. It is a beautiful step forward.*

With friendly greeting,

Yours,
A. Einstein

His paper had been translated into German by Albert Einstein himself and published in *Zeitschrift für Physik* with the note: 'In my opinion, Bose's derivation signifies an important advance.

The method used here gives the quantum theory of an ideal gas as I will work out elsewhere.'

Bose had succeeded in making significant contributions to the statistical foundation of quantum mechanics, whose importance was understood by Einstein from the documents he had sent.

Chapter Seven

By the time the response from Einstein came to Bose, the latter had written a second letter, on 15 June 1924. It contained his second paper.

> *Respected Master,*
>
> *I send herewith another paper of mine for your kind perusal and opinion. I hope my first paper has reached your hands. The result to which I have arrived seems rather important (to me at any rate). You will see that I have dealt with the problem of thermal equilibrium between Radiation and Matter in a different way, and have arrived at a different law for the*

probability for elementary processes, which seems to have simplicity in its favour. I have ventured to send you the type-written paper in English. It being beyond me to express myself in German (which will be intelligible to you), I shall be glad if its publication in Zeitschrift fur Physik *or any other German journal can be managed. I myself know not how to manage it. In any case, I shall be grateful if you express your opinion on the papers and send it to me at the above address.*

Yours truly,
S.N. Bose

~

Albert Einstein's endorsement of Satyendranath Bose's work made the latter a star. Bose had made a pathbreaking contribution. Not only was his own work important and recognized by Einstein, Bose had laid the foundation over which many significant works have been carried out subsequently by scientists all over the world.

How was Satyendranath Bose's work significant? He carried out a statistical calculation for the kind of particles that later came to be named after him—'bosons'. He presented an alternative derivation for the radiation law earlier found by Max Planck. After Einstein translated and published Bose's work, the former predicted that when a given number of particles approach each other 'sufficiently closely and move sufficiently slowly', they will together convert to the lowest energy state—what is now termed the Bose-Einstein condensation (BEC).

Bose's name is now associated closely with Einstein. The BEC was first observed through experiments in 1995 in alkali atom gases. Eric A. Cornell, Wolfgang Ketterle and Carl E. Wieman were awarded the Nobel Prize in Physics in 2001, for experiments derived from the work that Bose and Einstein did seventy years before.

This was their finding: the air around us consists of particles that are constantly moving at several hundred metres per second. The lower the temperature, the slower the pace of the particles. Earlier, it was thought that the temperature that led to the formation of the BEC cannot be reached on Earth. But these scientists were able to do this in alkali atom gases.

British physicist Paul Dirac was the first to use the term 'boson' to describe the particles that followed Bose-Einstein statistics. The naming celebrated Bose's contribution to developing the theory. When a work is pathbreaking, it shows new directions and leads to many more new findings. Bose's work was like that.

~

Satyen Bose loved to teach, but he did not not want to confine himself for the rest of his life in Dhaka University. He was restless. He wanted to be in Europe, where so many new discoveries were being made. Satyen longed to explore new possibilities, to use top-class laboratories and libraries, listen to renowned scientists read out their papers, and to discuss scientific matters and explore possibilities of collaborative work with some of them.

He wanted to be where these things were

actually happening, instead of sitting in Dhaka, which was so far away from it all!

He had applied for a leave of two years from Dhaka University. Would it be granted by the authorities with whom he was already having differences over his contract and salary?

Chapter Eight

After the endorsement from Albert Einstein, Satyendranath Bose's application for leave of two years from his teaching job at Dhaka University was granted easily, and he was also given an allowance. He was finally ready to explore new possibilities.

His first destination was Paris. Bose first went to Bombay, and from there sailed to reach Paris in October 1924. He had many friends living in the city at that point. He headed to 17 Rue du Sommerard. Satyen's friend from school, Girijapati Bhattacharjee, was in Paris at that time.

Within a week of reaching Paris, Satyen Bose wrote to Einstein, explaining that he was keen on working with him. He thanked him for translating his paper to German and for the effort that he took to get it published. He also mentioned his second paper that he had sent to Einstein. The second paper had been published by then, but Bose did not know about it. He learnt it from Einstein, who also added that he did not agree with him on it and explained to him the reason.

This, naturally, disappointed Satyen, who had great expectations from this paper as well. Satyen began to work on the areas pointed out by Einstein and wrote a third paper.

Satyen wrote to Einstein:

The views about the radiation field, which I have ventured to put forward, seem to be very much like what Bohr has recently expressed in May Phil. Mag. 1924. But it is only a guess, as I cannot say honestly to have exactly understood all he means to say, about virtual fields and virtual oscillators.

I am rather anxious to know your opinion about it. I have shown it to Professor Langevin here and he seems to think it interesting and worth publishing...

However, this third paper was neither published nor found in the Einstein archives. It has remained untraceable. Langevin, who is mentioned in the letter, was French scientist Paul Langevin, who richly contributed to various areas in physics. Langevin was then the Director of the institution where radium was discovered.

Satyen had been in Paris now for a few months. But the Indian students there had absolutely no idea yet about his work, and that Albert Einstein himself had translated his paper and the work itself was pathbreaking. Even a close friend like Girijapati had no idea.

On a cold February morning of 1925, Girijapati realized that it had snowed all night and it would be impossible to go out that day. He made his way to Satyen's room, to chat with him and spend the day with his friend.

He knocked on the door.

'Entré vous!' came the response.

Satyen was on the bed, reading Dante's *The Divine Comedy* in Italian. Seeing Girija, a delighted Satyen ordered two cups of hot chocolate and croissants.

'I have a small gift for you, Girija,' Satyen said after some time.

'What is it?' Girija said, enthused. 'An interesting book?'

Satyen handed over a German publication. Girija knew only rudimentary German, so Satyen explained it to him. He narrated the story on the note written by Albert Einstein that said: 'Bose's method of derivation of Planck's Law, in my opinion, signifies a forward step. The method applied here yields the Quantum theory of ideal gases as I will show elsewhere.' The copies of some reprints of the published work had just reached him the day before.

'A forward step! Said by Albert Einstein

about *your* work! This is momentous, my friend!' Girija said, getting up from the seat and pacing excitedly around the room. 'Why didn't you tell me before?' he asked. 'This is unbelievable!' He was delirious with joy. A shy smile played on his lips, but Satyen remained as calm as ever, and went back to his book.

Around this time, Satyen met Marie Curie. He was introduced to her by Paul Langevin, who was a former student of her husband and partner in research, Pierre Curie. Pierre and Marie Curie had received half of the Nobel Prize for Physics in 1903 for their study of radioactivity discovered by Henri Becquerel, who was awarded the other half of the Prize.

Satyen Bose was keen to work at Marie Curie's Radium Institute on radioactivity. He

carried with him a letter of introduction from Langevin. Marie read the letter and said she could not refuse a person who had got such a recommendation. 'But not right now, after three or four months. Get to know the language, otherwise you will find it difficult to work in the lab,' she told him in English.

Satyen listened to her intently but did not get the opportunity to tell her that he knew French already and had been learning the language for over ten years. Later, he worked at the Radium Institute for some time.

Marie Sklodowska was born in Warsaw in 1867. In 1891, Marie moved to Paris to study Physics and Mathematical Sciences at the Sorbonne. There, she met Pierre Curie who was professor in the School of Physics, and married him in 1895.

Marie became the Head of the Physics Laboratory at the Sorbonne, got her Doctor of Science degree in 1903, and became a Professor of General Physics in the Faculty of Sciences. She was the first woman to hold this position. She was also appointed Director of the Curie Laboratory in the Radium Institute of the University of Paris.

The discovery of radioactivity by Henri Becquerel in 1896 led the Curies to research in the field and examine many elements for their radioactivity. Their findings led them to extract two unknown substances—polonium and radium. Both of these were more radioactive than uranium. Marie and

Pierre were awarded half of the Nobel Prize for Physics in 1903. In 1911, she received a second Nobel Prize, this time in Chemistry. She became the first person to receive two Nobel Prizes. She died in France in 1934.

After a year in Paris, it was time for Satyen Bose to go to Berlin. It was October 1925. Albert Einstein was living here then. Bose was happy to learn that almost everyone had read his paper here, and were discussing it. He was given access to all scientific institutions and government libraries.

He met many scientists. He was a keen observer and learner, and attended many seminars and learned various developments. He read constantly, happy that he had access to libraries and did not have to pay fees or submit deposits for the time he spent there. This was a great honour and privilege that he greatly valued. He was also given easy access to the laboratories which few people could enter. All this was an acknowledgment of the groundbreaking work he had done. He also interacted with brilliant minds like Walter Bothe, Peter Debye, Wolfgang Pauli, Otto Hahn, Werner Heisenberg and many others during these two years. Many new things were happening in Berlin around that time that drew scientists from all over the world to the city.

Satyen Bose visited Albert Einstein often and had long discussions on various matters not just about science. They also talked about politics and how deeply it affected their lives.

During a discussion, Einstein told Bose: 'I think Englishmen are better than other Western colonial nations, and I think they are better than the French and the Dutch. You should not be surprised at a German like me praising the English [especially after World War I in which these two nations were fighting against each other]. Now, tell me, do you really want the British to quit your country?'

'Of course!' said Satyen. He had no doubt about it. 'We all want to determine our own destinies.'

But Einstein wasn't convinced. He wanted to press Satyen further to understand this. 'Suppose there was a button near you and all the Englishmen would quit India if you were to press it. Would you press that button?'

'If God were to grant me such an opportunity, I will not hesitate even for a moment to press it.'

'Really?' asked Einstein. He kept quiet for a few moments. Satyen now asked a question that would make his reason clear.

'Why do you Jews then want to establish a new state? You seem to be fairly inclined in its favour,' Satyen said. Satyen was right. Einstein understood this time.

'Of course. I can now understand what you are saying... it is an emotional matter and cannot be understood rationally.'

~

In 1926, Satyen Bose's two years of study leave got over, and he left Germany. Einstein remained in Berlin till 1933. After the Nazis seized power in

Germany, Einstein moved to the US and worked at the Institute for Advanced Study in Princeton. Many other scientists Bose knew closely had to leave Germany as well.

Around the time of his return, there was an opening at Dhaka University for the position of Professor and Head of the Department of Physics. But there was a problem: Satyendranath Bose did not have a doctorate. It was then that Albert Einstein wrote a letter of recommendation for him. On 16 March 1926, Einstein wrote:

> *The recent works of Mr S.N. Bose, especially his theory of radiation equilibrium, signify in my opinion an important and enduring progress of the physical theory. Also, in personal discussion with Mr Bose, I have got the impression that he is a man of unusual*

gift and depth, from whom science has much to expect. He has also at his command an extensive knowledge and certain ability in our science. As university teacher he will certainly develop a successful and prosperous activity.

The post was still offered to another professor. When he turned it down, it was offered to Satyendranath Bose. That year, he was also made the Dean of Science.

Chapter Nine

Satyendranath Bose now began to use his rich experiences in Europe to improve Dhaka University. He was also working on making his own experimental equipment. He collaborated with other scientists over the next few years and wrote papers that were published in renowned scientific journals. More and more, he came to be known as a renowned scientist, a brilliant teacher and a person who backed his students and encouraged them.

In 1928, Bose went to Calcutta where he met

C.V. Raman. It is said that Bose told Raman that day: 'Professor Raman, you have made a great discovery. It will be called the Raman Effect and you will get the Nobel Prize.' And it turned out to be true!

This was a time of brilliant breakthroughs in the field of science by Indians. Meghnad Saha's equation of thermal ionisation, the Bose statistics, the Raman effect by C.V. Raman—all went on to have long-lasting impacts.

As a teacher, Bose was always encouraging and supportive of his students. He pushed them to do experiments and to excel in various fields, not just restricting their interest in the subject they were pursuing academically. Satyendranath Bose was himself interested in various subjects and encouraged his own students to be enthusiastic about everything happening around them.

Things began to change in Dhaka in the 1930s. India continued to be under British rule, but the political situation was changing every day. Political disturbances and communal riots had a devastating effect on the lives of ordinary people. It was only a matter of time that trouble entered colleges and university campuses across the country. Dhaka had always been a centre of learning but riots broke out in 1941, and classes remained suspended for long.

Bose had been getting offers to return to Calcutta, but had turned them down. Gradually, as the situation in Dhaka was no longer the same, he decided it may be a good time to return 'home' to Calcutta. Despite the reluctance of

Dhaka University to let go of him, he was keen on returning to the city of his birth and where he had spent his childhood and youth.

Dr Bidhu Bhushan Roy, a pioneer in the field of X-ray spectroscopy, had set up an X-ray laboratory in Calcutta—arguably the first of its kind in India—after gaining rich experience in the lab of Niels Bohr in Copenhagen. When

Roy died suddenly in 1944, Vice Chancellor Shyamaprasad Mookerjee asked Satyendranath Bose to consider the offer at the University College of Science and Technology. Satyen Bose returned to Calcutta after twenty-five years.

Satyendranath Bose had always been informal. His door was always open for those who wished to work with him. Many students and young professionals joined his study circle—an informal academic session that was held every weekend.

Meghnad Saha was then teaching in the physics department of University College and very soon, right after the country's Independence, he would set up an institute of nuclear physics, in 1949.

Satyen Bose continued his experiments in

crystallography and radiation physics with young students. New fields of research were coming up such as minerals and clays. Bose was always curious about new things and was obsessed with problem solving. He and his students worked on setting up an X-ray laboratory that became a centre for crystal structure analysis.

He travelled widely, including Europe, became President of the Indian Physical Society (1945), President of the National Institute of Sciences (1948), and was nominated a member of the Rajya Sabha and honoured with the Padma Vibhushan, the second-highest civilian award in India. He also became Vice Chancellor of Viswa Bharati in 1956. Meanwhile, he published five papers related to the Unified Field Theory.

In 1955, Albert Einstein died, just months

ahead of an international conference in Bern to mark the fiftieth year of the special theory of relativity. Bose was expecting to meet him there again, but it did not happen.

It was also around this time that his dear friend Meghnad Saha died on 16 February 1956.

Satyen continued with his research work and never tired of expanding his vista. He continued to be thirsty for knowledge till the very end. He was very enthusiastic about a project involving the extraction of helium from the hot springs of Bakreswar that was first found by Professor Shyamadas Chatterjee.

During the later part of his life, Satyen Bose was keen about using Bengali as a medium of teaching science in schools and colleges in

Bengal. He felt that students could grasp a subject better and 'naturally' if they learned it in their mother tongue. It would then make a person progress faster instead of getting entangled in the difficulties of a foreign language.

His views were criticised and opposed by many as they felt it was impractical in India where people spoke in so many languages. Common grounds of discussion and research was impossible in regional languages, they said, but Bose firmly believed that language was becoming a barrier in learning. He spoke on the issue several times in public speeches and in his writings. He often taught in the Bengali language and delivered speeches on important occasions in it.

He helped form the Bangiya Vijnan Parishad

(Bengal Science Society) in 1947-48, with the objective of making science popular through the Bengali language. The organization published a journal called *Jnan O Vijnan*.

Satyen Bose loved his addas a great deal. After returning to Calcutta, he would have regular gatherings at his Ishwar Mill Lane home. In the last few years of his life, he translated many works from French, German and Italian. He was greatly drawn to music all his life and played the esraj and the flute. Like many renowned scientists, Satyendranath too had a flair for music. Music could literally move him to tears. Over years of listening and practicing, he had developed a rather eclectic taste in music—he listened to everything from folk to classical, Indian to Western.

Satyendranath Bose died on 4 February 1974, a few weeks after he turned eighty.

Bose's findings have been etched in history and have led to many significant findings. According to Abraham Pais, physicist and biographer of Einstein, 'The paper by Bose is the fourth and last of the revolutionary papers of the old quantum theory, the other three being by Planck, Einstein and Bohr.' Bose began to be regarded as the 'originator of quantum statistics and an important figure behind quantum mechanics and quantum field theory'.

Many scientists feel that Satyendranath Bose should have received the Nobel Prize as his work was indeed pioneering. He had been nominated too. It is recorded that the Nobel Committee had asked its expert Oskar Klein in 1956 to evaluate Bose's work, and he had observed that while it was important, it was 'not so distinguished as the work of other physicists' who had won the prize.

But Satyendranth Bose himself never regretted it, and was happy and content with the love and recognition that he had received from so many people all over the world.

Explained by a Scientist

By Professor Shiraz Minwalla, as told to Swati Sengupta

What were the four papers by Albert Einstein published in 1905 about?

Albert Einstein's first paper was about the **photoelectric event**. It contributed to the development of quantum mechanics.

What Einstein looked at was: suppose you shine light on a substance, then it is experimentally observed that the light can sometimes knock out an electron from the substance. This is not very surprising because light carries energy. Electrons (which, in their normal state, are trapped in the substance) can absorb some light, and use the absorbed energy to escape—fly away from—the substance. According to classical physics, the ability of the light to knock an electron out of the substance is determined largely by its energy density (more precisely its intensity). Now the intensity of a classical wave is proportional to the square of its amplitude (how 'high' the wave is). For this reason, a classical physicist would have predicted that very high amplitude waves, of absolutely any frequency (no matter how small) would carry enough 'punch' to knock electrons out of any substance.

However, it was experimentally observed that light manages to knock electrons out only when its frequency is larger than a certain minimum. If the frequency of the light is smaller than this minimum, it is unable to knock electrons out, no matter how large is its amplitude (and hence its intensity).

Einstein explained all of this by proposing that light, in the quantum theory, actually comes in little packets called quanta or photons. And each quantum has an energy proportional to the frequency of the light. The proportionality constant, 'h', in this formula, is called Planck's constant (named after physicist Max Planck). The really crucial point is that electrons can only absorb either a full photon or nothing. The probability that the same electron can absorb more than one photon is so small that it can be ignored. From this new point of view, when one increases the intensity of light of a given frequency, one increases the number of photons (per unit area per unit time) incident upon the substance. But since any given electron absorbs at most one photon, it can absorb enough energy to escape the substance only if the energy of a single photon is large enough. But we have seen that the energy of a single photon is determined solely by its frequency. So, light with frequency below a certain minimum will be incapable of ejecting electrons from a substance, independent of the intensity of the light shone on the substance. This is precisely in line with what is observed. Moreover, since electrons absorb no more than one photon, the energy with which they are ejected is determined solely by the frequency of the incident light, and is independent of its intensity. This was the content of the paper that got him the Nobel Prize and contained a fundamental insight into the nature of reality.

Einstein's second paper was on **Brownian motion**. This can be explained simply: if you put something small, say a bacterium, in a glass of water and watch it under a microscope, you will observe that the particle doesn't just sit there but constantly moves around in a random manner. The reason this happens is that the molecules of water constantly bombard this particle from all sides making it jiggle around. Einstein worked out a quantitative theory of this jiggling. The importance of this theory was the following. In the early 1900s, the theory that matter was made up of atoms and molecules was still controversial. Einstein explained that the jiggling motion described above was direct visual evidence for the existence of molecules.

Einstein's formula could also be used to provide a quantitative estimate of the so-called Avagadro's number—the number of water molecules contained in 18 gm of water. This works as follows. If Avagadro's number was very very large, each water molecule would be very light, and so each collision would give the bacterium only a small kick. The number of such collisions per second, would, however, be very large. As water molecules collide from all sides, the net effect of these collisions would average out to nothing. If, on the other hand, Avagadro's number was smaller, there would be fewer collisions per unit time, and each collision would be more impactful, giving rise to observable random motion. Einstein demonstrated that the average distance travelled by a bacterium, in unit time, is proportional to one over the square root of Avagadro's number. Quantitative measurements of Brownian motion could, thus, be used to compute Avagadro's number, and give a value in agreement with previous estimates from the kinetic theory of gases. This quantitative agreement very convincingly demonstrated the reality of the molecular hypothesis.

Papers three and four were about the **Special Theory of Relativity**. These papers—together with his papers on the General Relativity—are Einstein's most important contributions to physics. Einstein explained that space and time are not as different as they appear to be. This can be understood with an analogy. Recall that space has three dimensions—this is simply the observation that there are three directions (left-right, front-back, up-down) in which you can move in space. Now, we may think that up and down are pretty different from left and right. This seems to be the case on Earth, because we fall downwards, not (for instance) to the left. We see this difference because we are on Earth. If we were out in empty space, far from all stars and planets, we would simply float around, not falling in any direction. It would then be clear to us that, at the fundamental level, all directions are on an equal footing. Mathematically we can say this in the following language. Imagine that you set up an x y z axis, and your friend sets up a second such coordinate system which differs from yours by a rotation. You and your friend would not agree on the values of the x y and z coordinates of points. However, the laws of geometry and physics take the same form when formulated in either of your coordinate systems.

Einstein realized that this basic principle is deeper than originally suspected. It extends to a principle of rotation not just in space but between space and time. Two different observers that are in different states of motion see space and time differently, because, roughly speaking, their space-time axes are rotated with respect to each other. While these two observers would not agree on the value of the spatial and time coordinates of events, however, they would both agree on the form of the laws of physics.

The fact that observers in relative motion do not agree on the value of the time coordinate of events is already a surprise. It implies that two events that seem simultaneous to one observer are not simultaneous to a second moving observer. Also, time runs in different rates for people who are moving in different speeds. Einstein's Special Relativity represents a fundamental—and completely unexpected—insight into the nature of reality.

In the fourth paper, Einstein showed that Special Relativity had the following major consequence. It implies that a particle that has some mass, automatically carries a related amount of energy. The value of this energy is given by the famous formula $E=mc^2$.

What was Satyendranath Bose's finding and how was it significant?

Satyendranath Bose's first paper that he sent to Einstein was a very important, fundamental and significant piece of work.

In thermodynamics we ask questions about probabilities. We could, for instance, ask for the probability that a certain particle is in a particular state ('state' means 'doing something').

Prior to quantum mechanics, it had been assumed that if you have a bunch of particles and they are interacting weakly, then what one particle is doing is independent of what the other particle is doing. So, the probability that a bunch of particles are simultaneously doing something can be obtained by multiplying the probability of the first particle being in its state, the second particle being in its state and so on. This reasonable-sounding assumption was the basis of the statistical theory built by James Clerk Maxwell and others.

Now, within quantum mechanics, it turns out that fundamental particles are of two sorts: 'bosons' or 'fermions.' And these fundamental particles are identical to one another. So, if let's say, photon number 1 occupies state number 1 and photon number 2 occupies state number 2, that's exactly the same state, the same configuration as photon number 1 occupying state number 2 and photon 2 occupying state 1. According to the earlier rule, these two configurations would have been regarded as two different states. Bose realized this is the wrong way to think.

One should not attempt to keep track of which particle is occupying which state, but only of how many particles are in any given state. If, say, five photons are in state number 1, that's all you need to say. It is not meaningful to specify which photons occupy this state. This was the key point. Bose translated this way of thinking into some rather simple mathematics. He postulated that the usual laws of statistical physics work as they always did but with this new rule for counting states.

Now with this rule and other postulates [like the quantisation of photons (light comes in packets)], Bose could very simply recover the Planck blackbody formula. This important formula was discovered by Planck around 1900, and led to the birth of quantum mechanics.

If you apply the usual rules of statistical physics to the classical electromagnetic field, you very quickly come to a contradiction. Say, you take a box and heat it up to some temperature, and ask how much energy is contained in the form of radiation. Using classical electrodynamics plus statistical mechanics, you'll get the answer 'infinity'. And the infinity comes from the fact that statistical mechanics predicts that there is an infinite amount of energy in very, very short wavelength or very, very high frequency photons. This answer is of course ridiculous because when you do an experiment, you don't get infinite energies. Planck produced a formula that correctly computed the amount of energy in radiation, but his formula needed a justification. An important element in the justification of

Planck's formula comes from the fact that light comes in discrete packets called photons. But to get all the details right one needs to correctly count the states of these photons. Bose's way of counting immediately gives the correct answer for Planck's formula. This very important and strikingly simple point had been missed by the physics community for a long time.

What was the content of the second paper Bose sent to Einstein? Why did Einstein not agree with it?

Einstein and others predicted that if an atom were to emit a photon into a state that already contains 'n' photons, then the probability that happens is increased by the factor n+1. In other words, photons like to be emitted into states that are already occupied by lots of other photons. In modern times this phenomenon has a striking experimental verification in the phenomenon of lasers.

In this second paper, Bose attempted to challenge the rule described above. He also proposed a new rule to replace Einstein's rule.

Einstein's objection to Bose's ideas was the following. He pointed out that Bose's rule implies that while external photons play a key role in inducing transition of an atomic state from a lower to a higher energy, the presence of photons outside had no effect on the rate of the reverse transitions (i.e. from a higher to a lower energy). While this feature may, at first, sound intuitively plausible (external photons are needed for the absorption of energy, they don't seem relevant for a process that releases energy), Einstein pointed out that cannot be correct. It violates a fundamental postulate of the quantum theory, namely that the 'transition amplitude' of going from state A to state B is the same as the transition amplitude for going from state B to state A. Einstein's own rule respected this principle. It is now completely clear that Einstein was correct.

Satyendranath Bose:
A Timeline

- 1 January 1894: Satyendranath Bose born in Calcutta to Surendranath Bose and Amodini Debi.
- 1913: Passed B.Sc. from Presidency College, Calcutta.
- 1914: Satyendranath gets married to Ushabati Ghose.
- 1915: Passes M.Sc. from Presidency College, Calcutta.

- 1916 to 1921: Is a lecturer in the Department of Physics, University of Calcutta.
- 1921: Joins Department of Physics in the newly opened Dacca University (now in Bangladesh, called University of Dhaka), as a Reader.
- 1924: Writes a paper 'Planck's Law and the Light-Quantum Hypothesis' and sends it to *Philosophical Magazine*. When there is no response, he sends it to Albert Einstein in Germany. Einstein himself translates it to German and gets it published in the prestigious journal *Zeitschrift für Physik*. Bose leaves for two years on a study trip to Europe.
- 1926: Returns to Dhaka, becomes Professor and Head of the Department of Physics.
- 1945: Returns to Calcutta to teach at Calcutta University.

- 1954: Satyendranath Bose is conferred with India's second highest civilian award, Padma Vibhushan.
- 1956: Retires and is made Professor Emeritus of Calcutta University (in 1958).
- 1956: He is appointed Vice Chancellor of Vishwa Bharati University, Shantiniketan.
- 1958: Satyendranth Bose became a Fellow of the Royal Society.
- 4 February 1974: Satyendranath Bose dies in Calcutta.

Author's Note

This book would not have been possible without the help and support of physicist Shiraz Minwalla, and author and editor Ananya Dasgupta. Shiraz explained Albert Einstein and S.N. Bose's scientific theories in a way that can be easily grasped by young readers. The section 'Explained by a Scientist' is by Shiraz Minwalla, Distinguished Professor in the Department of Theoretical Sciences at the Tata Institute of Fundamental Research, Mumbai.

To write this book, I primarily referred to

S.N. Bose: The Man and His Work, Part II Life, Lectures and Addresses, Miscellaneous Pieces (1994, S.N. Bose National Centre for Basic Sciences, Calcutta, Editors C.K. Majumdar, Partha Ghose, Enakshi Chatterjee, Sarnik Bandyopadhyay and Santimay Chatterjee). The book offers deep insight into Bose's life and work. I also referred to articles such as 'Einstein Revealed As Brilliant In Youth', by Walter Sullivan, published in the *New York Times*, 14 February 1984, and 'Remembering the Life of Satyendra Nath Bose' by Amitabha Bhattacharya in the *Economic & Political Weekly*, 6 April 2019, among many others.

For several simplified definitions of complex scientific terms, nobelprize.org, aip.org and nationalgeographic.com were very helpful.

Thank you Mita Dastidar and Sreyashi Dastidar for explaining some important terms during S.N. Bose's times, and to Sriparna Ray and Bitanu Chatterjee for their support. I am grateful to Sudeshna Shome Ghosh for asking me to do this series that now has eight books and has been a delightful learning experience. Thank you Devashish Verma for the fabulous illustrations.

Swati Sengupta

HAVE YOU READ ALL THE *INCREDIBLE LIVES* BOOKS?

The Incredible Life of Milkha Singh: The Runner Who Could Fly

He was an athlete who overcame life's odds to become one of India's greatest sporstpersons. This is his inspiring story of grit and determination.

In a small village in Punjab, little Milkha Singh grew up, loved by his parents, surrounded by open fields where he could run, play, and fly kites. In the heat of summer, when he had to walk to school barefoot, he would run like the wind so he could get home fast. And then, one day, in the midst of terrible violence and upheaval, his family and home were snatched away forever. Milkha, still a teenager, found himself alone and friendless, till he was recruited into the Army. Here, he finally found his passion and joy—running.

The Incredible Life of Jhalkari Bai: The Braveheart Warrior

She was the bravest girl in her village. And one day, she became one of the bravest women her country had ever known.

Jhalkari Bai grew up in Bhojla, many miles away from the city of Jhansi. Far from the grand forts and palaces and illustrious kings and queens of Jhansi, in her village, she was known for her great strength and bravery—fighting off tigers and dacoits all alone. She nurtured a fierce desire to be a soldier, and to do amazing acts of courage. Today, Jhalkari Bai is present as just a footnote in history. But she lives on in the hearts of her people in Jhansi, Bhojla and beyond. This is her incredible and memorable story of bravery and sacrifice.

The Incredible Life of Birsa Munda:
The Great Revolutionary

He was a simple Adivasi boy. But one day he had to stand up and protest all the wrongs being done to his people. And so an unforgettable revolutionary was born.

Birsa Munda lived in one of the villages that dotted the Chhotanagpur region in today's Jharkhand. He was a dreamy boy with an uncanny ability to mesmerise not only humans but birds and animals too with his words and music. As he grew up, he became more and more aware of the exploitation of the Adivasi people by rich landowners and the British government. Birsa spoke out one day, and from that moment on, he started a journey that saw him become one of India's greatest tribal leaders and icons of resistance.

The Incredible Life of Savitribai Phule:
The Fearless Reformer

All she wanted was to be able to go to school. But she and many like her were denied this because of their caste. That did not stop her.

When she was nine years old, Savitri was married to thirteen-year-old Jyotirao Phule. Savitri yearned to be able to go to school, to read books. Jyotiba wanted his wife to be educated as well, and so he taught her. Soon, she learnt not just to read and write, but also trained as a teacher. Together, Savitribai and Jyotirao Phule started schools where girls and boys, dalit children, and those who had been shunned from schools till then could get educated. They fought against caste atrocities. They made sure that women learnt of their rights to exist with dignity.

The Incredible Life of Bhagat Singh:
The Indomitable Freedom Fighter

He had a burning desire to see India as an independent country. He would stop at nothing to make it happen.

Born in 1907 to a family of farmers in Punjab, Bhagat Singh at the age of three had declared that he was sowing guns so he could fight the British colonisers. As he grew up, Bhagat Singh became a widely read and fiercely intelligent man. He would dedicate his life to not only making India free but also towards creating a more equitable society.

The Incredible Life of Arati Saha:
The Swimmer Who Wouldn't Give Up

From the moment she learnt to swim, Arati set her eyes on difficult challenges. Then she decided to do what no Asian woman had done before—swim the English Channel.

Arati Saha was born in 1940, and learnt to swim in the Hooghly river in Calcutta as a child. At the age of eight, she competed in the National Championship in Bombay, winning silver and bronze medals. In 1952, she was selected as one of the first four women to represent independent India at the Helsinki Summer Olympics. At eleven years and ten months she was the youngest Indian Olympian—a record that stands till this day. By the time she was eighteen, Arati was looking for a fresh challenge—she decided to swim the English Channel.

The Incredible Life of Anandibai Joshee:
The Girl Who Fought to Be a Doctor

Little Anandi was a strong and intelligent girl. Faced with tragedy as a child bride, she was determined to study to be a doctor and save lives.

Anandi led a very different life from other girls of the times. Her husband wanted her to study and made sure she could attend school. At the age of twelve, faced with a terrible loss, Anandi decided to become a doctor so she could help others. And she wanted to do so by going to faraway United States.